CTHULHU SENRYU

NICK MAMATAS

PRIME BOOKS

CTHULHU SENRYU

Copyright © 2006 by **Nick Mamatas.**

Cover art © 2006 by **Frank Wu.**

Prime Books

www.prime-books.com

1. Do you want to be
down with the elder gods, son?
Eat squid, take a nap.

2. H.P. Lovecraft was
one very fucked up writer.
I stole his ideas.

3. R'lyeh has stop lights.
A mournful red glow means stop.
Elder sign means die.

4. Jack Kerouac could
kick a shoggoth's blob ass.
Count on it, bub.

5. There sure are a lot
of mythos titles out there.
Largely owned by nerds.

6. In dear old R'lyeh
dead Cthulhu lies dreaming
Pretty soggy too.

7. Azathoth, you rock
I bob my head for all time
to eldritch Muzak

8. This poem contains
the weird unheard word squamous
and is also cursed

9. Thank you for buying
this limited edition.
You're doomed anyway

10. Necronomicon!
a very entertaining
read, nine thumbs way up

11. Clark Ashton Smith was
a much better writer than
Ol' H. P. Lovecraft

12. I am Providence
reads Lovecraft's tombstone, right? Mine?
I am Long Island.

13. At the mountains of
madness I met my true love.
Her name lost to me.

14. Doctor Herbert West
re-animator and an
ears, nose, and throat man

15. That is not dead which
can eternal lie and with
aaah, you know the rest

16. Poe, Lovecraft, Blackwood
the new six-man tag team champs
beat the Von Erichs

17. Mind if I re-write
your stuff, August asked H. P.
but after he died

18. The doom that came to
Sarnath was real estate
gentrification

19. "The Colour out of
Space" is my favorite one
Which one do you like?

20. Howard, dude! Really!
Cool it with the racism.
Don't be an asshat.

21. "The Dunwich Horror"
Holy Christ, did the movie
version suck or what?

22. Did you get the call?
The damned call of Cthulhu
Or did the voicemail?

23. Miskatonic U.
gave me a big scholarship
but I went to Brown

24. When the stars are right
all hell will break loose. 'Til then,
keep on truckin', friends!

25. Tentacles sought to
crush my very soul, but I
prepared Greek salad

26. Nyarlathotep.
So cool I have to shout it
NYARLATHOTEP!

27. Believe in old gods?
Not H. P. Lovecraft, a pure
materialist.

28. For sale on eBay:
sunken monolith of Gnoph.
Shipping costs were high.

29. Blasphemes and bubbles
all the live-long day, doo-dah
doo-dah, Azathoth!

30. Dagon, the Fish-God
fought the American Dream.
He became fish sticks.

31. Iridescent cones
ten feet tall, four arms as well!
This is the Great Race?

32. Iron Chef prepared
five great dishes with the theme
fungi from Yuggoth

33. I saw a shoggoth
it changed shape, a swirling mass
or was it Oprah?

34. "Tsathoggua!" I cried.
"God bless you," Jerry said back.
He's a damn wise guy.

35. The goat of the woods
with a thousand young is here!
What's she doing here?

36. The Great Old Ones want
you for the Dreamland Army.
Earn money for school!

37. Yog-Sothoth in my
peanut butter, and peanut
butter in my Yog.

38. Charles Dexter Ward
does not know what he's in for.
He will take the case.

39. The great flapping wings
of the Mi-Go, where they fly
you don't want to go

40. Innsmouth, a good place
to raise spoiled kids and then
sacrifice them all.

41. Nuke Cthulhu, he just
rematerializes
five minutes later.

42. Your arms are too short
to box with The Great Old Ones,
Charlie Brown. Oh drat.

43. An underrated
story like "The Silver Key"
is worth a re-read

44. Supernatural
Horror in Literature
could use an update

45. Can you hear that voice?
The Whisperer In Darkness?
Speak up, would ya, pal?

46. The plush Cthulhu.
What's next? Saturday morning
cartoons, cereal?

47. Ever read a Beat
poem? How about one in
the mode of Lovecraft?

48. Horror at Red Hook?
Hey pal, my father works there.
He's a longshoreman.

49. I submit stories
to Weird Tales but it's just not
the same anymore.

50. Jack Kerouac is
the hero of this novel.
Lovecraft is the God.

51. Realist novels
are very boring to me.
Lovecraft was better.

52. In Cthulhu fandom
if a big nerd corners you
simply smile and nod.

53. The Antarctic is so cold
and so very ancient too.
Mountains of madness.

54. Signed and numbered, signed
and numbered, a poem would
break monotony.

55. Night Shade Books paid a
small advance for this novel.
I'm happy with it.

56. Quiet dignity.
That was old H. P. Lovecraft.
The king of the nerds.

57. Lovecraft, a stellar penpal.
Seventy-page letters were
not that uncommon.

58. William S. Burroughs
was a student of Barlow.
That's the missing link.

59. On the road again.
Running from monsters all day.
It still beats working.

60. Jack K. wrote haiku.
Lovecraft didn't write any.
That sure is a shame.

61. They fixed Lovecraft's tales.
Eliminated Derleth.
Joshi did it well.

62. Arkham House did good.
Kept Lovecraft's stories in print.
But they fucked some up.

63. Lovecraft wanted to
attend Brown. He never could,
but his papers did.

64. Amateur writer.
He worked to go pro but there's
no money in pulps

65. I see racialist
fears in "The Shadow Over
Innsmouth"; wrecks the text

66. Kingsport to Arkham
ride the trolley for a dime
but never return.

67. Infintesimal,
our place in the universe.
Entertaining, no?

68. The Old Ones made life
by accident or in jest.
Thanks for the favor.

69. I like adjectives.
Lots of 'em and adverbs too.
So I read Lovecraft.

70. On "The Curse Of Yig"
I will tell you this one thing
Walker deserved it.

71. Cthulhu is my
homeboy, I call him Cuthie
for short. What it is.

72. Lovecraft was married.
But he didn't love his wife
all that much, did he?

73. Ernest Hemingway
was a contemporary.
They never hung out.

74. Proust, Joyce, Spengler, Freud.
They're in Lovecraft's library.
But are they in yours?

75. Sonia Greene describes:
"adequately excellent
lover." Damn, Howard!

76. Lovecraft wrote down his
dreams as dark tales fully formed.
What was he eating?

77. Jack Kerouac wrote
a fantasy novel once.
It's called Doctor Sax.

78. Neal Cassady
I wouldn't lend him money,
not if I were you.

79. Lovecraft did not like
what they called "Negro music"
but Kerouac did.

80. William S. Burroughs.
Shot his wife, then ran away.
The William Tell trick.

81.Join a Cthulhu cult.
It will give your life meaning.
Meaning: "You're a dork."

82. Jack and Howard P.
Dead authors lie sleeping, but
I still rip them off.

83. Do you like pastiche?
An experiment with words.
Or was this book lame?

84. I live in deep space.
I summer in New England.
Have you heard of me?

85. "Why don't you fuck off,"
said the fan to the author.
This is fucking off!

86. Three-lobed burning eye!
Take a look at that, Jesus!
He needs trifocals.

87. You know what is lame?
"Cthulhu For President!"
He wasn't even born here.

88. For my next trick I'll
cross Lovecraft and Bukowski.
Pre-order the book.

89. Shub-Niggurath was
a lumberjack, a mighty
lumberjack, boyo.

90. Bring on The Old Ones.
Trouble is my middle name.
It's clobbering time.

91. Who would win this fight?
Cthulhu versus Lenin.
It's a trick question.

92. fthagn, yes, fthagn
How many syllables are
there? Well, let's say two.

93. Cthulhu's pimp cup
It's sparkling with the bling bling.
Shoggoth booty, yo!

94. A reality
show, called Survivor: R'lyeh.
Survivors? Zero.

95. Lovecraft purists are
excellent readers but tend
to be lame critics.

96. Intergalactic
smackdowns are a'poppin, and
humanity dies.

97. Cannot correlate
the contents of this dark world
or find my damn socks

98. In my turgid dreams
I wrestle a tentacle
wake up in the distant past

99. It's haunted you know,
the Necronomicon is.
So is the bookmark.

100. One hundred poems.
This last one is for you, friend.
Limited print run.

These poems originally appeared on the signature sheets of the limited edition of the author's first novel, **Move Under Ground** (Night Shade Books, 2004). Several of the poems reference this edition, its publisher, and the limitation of that edition.

www.ingramcontent.com/pod-product-compliance
Lightning Source LLC
Chambersburg PA
CBHW030831060726
47590CB00004B/1486